# Yoni Healing

# Yoni Healing

a sacred feminine self-care guide

Rhian Kivits

LOVE ALCHEMIST

Disclaimer

The information in this book is presented in accordance with Rhian Kivits' personal opinions and beliefs. If you are concerned about your physical or mental well-being you are always advised to consult a physician, in the first instance. Spiritual and holistic healing is always considered complementary. Your choices are your own and you are always responsible for your own health and well-being.

*Rhian Kivits*

LOVE ALCHEMIST

This book is dedicated to all women. May the infinite magic of the Divine Feminine flow freely through us all.

—Rhian

# Contents

*Part Three* **Yoni Healing: The Practices**

# Author's

## message

I wrote this book so that women who'd like to practice their own Yoni self-care rituals don't have to trawl through the internet to pull together information about how to begin.

When I became curious about the range of modalities that would help me reconnect with, heal and explore my Divine Feminine aspect I was in process – recovering from a traumatic relationship history and many years of sexual disconnection. I was working through layers of shame and self-blame after recurrent miscarriage. I'd also birthed three children and undergone an assisted delivery as well as a caesarean. I was completely out of touch with my body.

Like many women, grief and trauma had led me to the feet of the Goddess. She reminded me that everything I desire and require resides within me. She re-orientated me towards my eternal responsibility to love and care for myself. Over time, She gently steered me away from external seeking and guided me home.

That was when I found myself standing before the mystical portal of Yoni, ready to walk the sacred path of embodiment.

At that moment, a simple, no-nonsense Yoni healing 101 would have been exactly what I needed.

I wanted to get started surrounded by my own home comforts, in my own emotional space. I wanted to take my time and to feel safe so that I could be confident about taking my process into my own hands. I wanted to learn how to meet my own intimate needs and to heal in ways that suited me. And I didn't want to feel like I had to be a fully-fledged Yogini or Tantrika before I was able to do it.

After being asked where to find written information about Yoni healing by so many of the women who walk through the doors of my professional practice, it seemed like a wise move for me to write this book. I wanted to empower you to start where you're at; to practice curiosity and self-compassion and to experience the profound physical and emotional shifts that Yoni healing can offer you.

But before you begin, I'd love to offer you one piece of advice – nobody is more qualified than YOU on the subject of YOU.

That's right – you are the greatest expert there could ever be when it comes to your body, your healing, your needs, your desires, your spiritual path and your journey in love and life.

Yoni healing is a powerful, pure form of self-initiation into your highest truth – the edict of the Divine Feminine. So allow yourself to be self-guided and your Inner Goddess will shine through. She's ready and waiting for you.

In love and service,

_Rhian_

# Your free gift

As a thank you for purchasing this book, you're being gifted access to Rhian's Yoni Healing Meditation package. Simply visit **bit.ly/yonibook** and enter your name and email to receive your login details and access the magic.

# Part One

## Yoni Healing
## What's It All About?

# Yoni
## symbolism

Yoni is the ancient Sanskrit word for the female genitalia and sexual reproductive organs – the vulva, vagina, ovaries and womb.

Sanskrit is the language of ancient India. Known as 'the language of the Gods' and 'the mother of all languages', it's the language of the Vedas – the scriptures of the Indo-Aryan spiritual tradition at the roots of Hinduism, Buddhism and Jainism.

The word Yoni alludes to so much more than just a part of the female body. When translated as 'source', 'origin', 'fountain', 'passage of birth' or 'sacred temple', we understand that there's something about the concept of Yoni that challenges us to look beyond the physical and understand its spiritual essence.

Yoni is symbolic of Shakti, the primordial Divine Feminine and all that she stands for – sacred space, the eternal spiral of nature and the power to create and recycle.

The Divine Feminine energy is encoded within ancient sacred geometry, like the Flower Of Life and the Vesica Piscis. Shakti shows up in nature as flowers, the sexual organs of plants, which explains why we often associate flowers like the rose, lotus and lily with the sweet mysteries of female sensuality and sexuality.

In our modern medicalised world where our connection, as women, to the Goddess feels like it has been severed or forgotten as a result of our conditioning or past experiences, the feminine modality of Yoni healing is a profound path of reconnection and remembering.

*The iron-rich waters of Glastonbury's Red Spring symbolise the blood of the Goddess. They flow in the Chalice Well gardens where the symbol of the Vesica Piscis can be found.*

You can never be separated from your true essence, Goddess. It's just who you are.

—Rhian

# Yoni
## healing

Just as the word Yoni helps us understand the sacred symbolism of the female sex organs, Yoni healing describes a set of holistic self-care practices that requires us to treat ourselves as sacred.

These practices all support the well-being of our female bodies while reconnecting us to our Divine Feminine aspect, so that we can embody the Goddess we've always longed to be.

Whether we've lost her, forgotten her or been disconnected from her through our experiences in love and life, Yoni healing helps us welcome our Goddess back home.

The practices detailed in this book are flexible and designed as self-guided, so that you can create your own Yoni healing rituals. Using this book as a guide, you'll be able to develop a supportive Yoni healing practice for yourself from a combination of modalities – Yoni Breath Meditation, Yoni Self-Massage, Yoni Reflexology, Yoni Egg Mastery and Yoni Steaming.

All these self-care practices are best enjoyed intuitively, according to personal preference. As we get to know ourselves more fully and we become in tune with ourselves and our organic nature, we may choose to adapt our choice of practices and make adjustments to the practices themselves so that they suit us perfectly.

**When in doubt, ask Yoni. She knows exactly what to do.**

—Rhian

# Why Yoni healing?

There are all kinds of reasons why women are drawn to Yoni healing. Our primary motivation may be physical or spiritual.

Many of us stumble across Yoni healing because we're on a journey of holistic health. A troublesome menstrual cycle, pregnancy problems, endocrine disorders, menopause symptoms or sexual issues and the mental and emotional challenges that sometimes appear alongside these ailments are often what motivate us to seek natural self-help solutions.

When conventional medicine doesn't seem to offer a fix, the impact of our struggles with feminine well-being can be devastating for our relationships, sex lives and even our career paths. Our self-expression, self-worth and confidence can be destroyed when we become distressed, defensive and self-destructive as a result of poor well-being.

The embodied, holistic approach of Yoni healing offers us the opportunity to consider our well-being from a new perspective. It helps us notice and interpret the messages our bodies are begging us to hear so that we can take action to rebalance body, mind and soul and finally claim our feminine vitality again.

Other women discover Yoni healing as an aspect of the feminine spiritual path. When we immerse ourselves in the Divine Feminine nuances of any ancient culture, engage in practices like meditation that elevate our personal growth or become curious about the mysteries of soul and spirit, it's inevitable that we'll eventually feel the flow of Shakti within us and hear her irresistible call.

When it happens this way, our own inner Goddess is guiding us home. She reminds us to reclaim our seat of power. She's inspiring us to remember how awakening, activating and nurturing our own physical bodies unlocks a portal to the source of womanly magic and wisdom that shapes the unique expression of who we truly are.

The best spiritual teachers always remind us that knowledge and power are inherent and originate within. If our Yoni is the sacred space where our Divine Feminine knowledge and power reside, then our ultimate invitation must be to stop seeking external solutions for our feminine healing and come back to ourselves. When we take personal responsibility for our healing, the transformation we experience is always profound.

Women deserve to enjoy optimum well-being, loving relationships and fulfilling sex. We can all channel the full capacity of our feminine power into every aspect of our lives when we have the desire and the tools to make it happen. When we honour, respect and nurture our Yoni, we unleash the ancient secret of the feminine magic that has laid dormant within us for so long.

# Benefits
## of Yoni healing

Our Yoni is so important from a holistic health perspective. Women's physical and mental health is a complex topic and we cannot take our ability to remain in balance for granted.

There are so many factors that contribute to the root causes of the common symptoms that affect millions of women, like painful periods, fertility issues, vaginal dryness, yeast infections or mood swings, for example.

Yoni healing tackles feminine symptoms and facilitates cleansing, detoxification and activation from a combination of three distinct perspectives that come together in an alchemical holistic mix.

* **Body** – we restore physical balance through gentle, natural holistic solutions.

* **Mind** – we restore emotional balance and boost vitality because Yoni healing practices lift our mood and raise our vibrational frequency.

* **Soul** – we lovingly reconnect with, express and embody the Goddess within and feel her presence moving through us.

The many physical benefits reported by women who enjoy Yoni healing practices include a reduction in menstrual problems and pelvic pain, hormone rebalance and the elimination of painful thrush. Many women also report greater sexual sensitivity, receptivity and pleasure, a higher sex drive and better orgasms after engaging in Yoni healing.

There are also some very attractive benefits for women on a journey of sexual healing. When Yoni healing contributes to the release of past sexual or relationship traumas and women feel free from the emotional blocks around sex created by the guilt or shame we carry, we can begin to embrace sexual confidence, a healthier body image, a stronger feminine identity and we become available for truly fulfilling intimate relationships.

# Body

Holistic practitioners suggest the impact of stress and trauma, poor diet and nutrition, a build-up of chemicals or medications in the body and other aspects of our modern lifestyle can quickly and easily take their toll upon us.

They believe that physical and emotional toxins can accumulate in our tissues, especially when our blood and lymph circulation is sluggish or our neurochemistry and hormones are not regulated, contributing to a lack of feminine well-being and vitality.

# Mind

Tantric and Taoist healers explain that when we've suffered any kind of pain or trauma in our sexual or relationship history, we can hold the residual energy in our Yoni, which eventually becomes congested and stagnant. Every sexual encounter leaves an emotional and energetic imprint upon us and over time this accumulates.

Trapped emotion in our Yoni makes us feel blocked. We lose our capacity to be vulnerable and intimate and feel unavailable for relationships or sexual pleasure. Our Yoni may feel unresponsive and numb or tense and closed. In the worst-case scenario, our Yoni can be painful or sore without any medical or physical explanation, leaving us feeling debilitated and sexually disconnected.

Women who are plagued with these kinds of inexplicable symptoms often end up fobbed off and silenced by the medical profession. Talking therapies can be helpful but, without embodied solutions, the healing often comes to a halt.

# Soul

Ancient Eastern teachings speak of the Yoni as a gateway to the Divine Feminine. A woman's sexual energy is rather like a magic potion that elevates her consciousness so that she can commune with the Divine when she infuses her spirituality with her physical sexual experience. If she chooses, she can allow a lover to ride that wave of spiritual bliss with her.

Tantrikas who've learned how to work consciously with their sexual energy have learned that sexual arousal and orgasm are peak states during which we can receive inspiration, Divine downloads or higher wisdom that we can harness to enrich our lives.

Connecting with our Yoni doesn't always have to be sexually focused, however. Just as the Yoni experience can lift us into magical, high, transcendent energies, it can also soothe, calm and centre us so that we can enter the void – the spiritual realm of the deep, dark feminine – where we discover our timeless capacity to release, transform and regenerate.

This is a space of 'being' as opposed to 'doing', a place where we feel held, comforted, soothed and loved. It is where we create, nurture and birth new ideas because it's where the root of all possibilities resides.

# Yoni
## awakening

When we lose touch with our Yoni or we've accumulated physical or emotional healing issues, it's as if our Yoni is fast asleep. We forget our Divine Feminine aspect and we switch off the sexy sparkle that used to radiate from our aura and shine through our eyes.

We also lose confidence and feel so disconnected from ourselves that our self-esteem becomes eroded. It's easy to slip into a self-critical mode, lose faith in our ability to attract lovers or tell ourselves that we have nothing to offer in relationships any more.

A sleeping Yoni usually feels numb, so we may also find

ourselves wondering why we're not feeling as much as we'd like to during sex. We wonder if we've lost our sensitivity or tell ourselves that perhaps we're just not as sensitive as other women seem to be. We become less sexually motivated and develop fear or avoidance of intimacy.

In the same way that we become disconnected from our Inner Child, the part of us that is eternally child-like, we become disconnected from our Yoni, the part of us that is eternally and profoundly feminine, as a result of neglect, rejection or abuse. Our Yoni may have cried herself to sleep or she may have had no choice but to switch off because she could no longer stand the pain.

When our Yoni is sleeping, it may be because the alternative has seemed too difficult and we haven't known how to approach awakening and healing ourselves or where to begin. Perhaps it's been easier to let our sleeping Yoni rest because we've told ourselves that we need to keep ourselves together for our work, our children or partner. We know that if we scratch the surface of our issues, the emotional reaction could be volcanic.

The good news is that when we practice Yoni healing our Yoni wakes up gently. Self-directed self-care means that we're able to work through our issues at our own pace and we remain in control of the process.

Slowly and steadily, we reconnect to ourselves and reactivate our sensitivity so that we can feel sexually confident, powerful and alive again. Lovingly, we set ourselves free from guilt and shame and start to buzz with feminine pride. We overcome our fear of intimacy and embrace sexual surrender on our own terms.

We even start to hear our Yoni speak the soulful, intuitive language of our feminine wisdom. She guides us and speaks loving Divine Feminine words of affirmation that we've been longing to hear. She communicates her desires loud and clear and becomes a channel for our deepest soul-level feminine expression.

Being really in touch with our awakened Yoni means that our sensual gateway is wide open, and we are ready to luxuriate in the love, honour and joy that we deserve. As we rediscover the huge range of pleasure sensations that our Yoni can offer us, we remember that our Yoni is the softest, most inviting, juiciest and most magical place in our bodies. We fall in love with her, sometimes for the very first time, and begin to feel true awe and wonder about ourselves, as women, again.

In fact, our Yoni is truly a powerhouse of creativity. When she's awake, we feel magnetic and we're motivated to deepen our existing relationships or welcome new love into our lives.

Yoni awakening also lays the foundations for truly alchemical sex – the kind of sex that feels like Heaven on Earth. And when we've consolidated our awakening and healing and we're ready to infuse Divine purpose into our sex, we can ritualise this alchemy and harness its power to manifest our highest desires.

This is known as the transmutation of sexual energy, or orgasmic manifesting. It's a timeless, feminine secret that can only be described as the ultimate expression of our feminine sovereignty and creative potential.

While the details of orgasmic manifesting don't fall within the scope of this book, having an awakened Yoni is a prerequisite for this magic. Being committed to healing and self-care is essential if we aspire to harness our magnificent womanly power.

**Awaken to Yoni, awaken to life.**

—Rhian

# Part Two

## Yoni Healing
## How To Prepare

# Yoni

## womb and moon

Women of all ages and at all stages of life can enjoy Yoni healing. In terms of choosing when to engage in healing practices, we must first listen to our body and our intuition.

Learning to act on our desire and to trust our inner voice is a feminine transferable skill that we can apply in every area of our lives, especially in our sex lives and relationships. It also helps us manage our families and our working lives in a state of flow rather than struggling against the tide, forcing ourselves to do things that don't feel right and fail to bring us joy and pleasure.

When we really want to do something, we're more

likely to succeed. When we have the desire to heal, we're more receptive to transformation. When we're inspired to engage in self-care practices they'll feel more personally meaningful.

However, this doesn't mean that we can allow our resistance to take over, keeping us feeling stuck in a place where we refuse to get started or driving us towards distractions and excuses that mean we won't make the time and create the space for self-care.

All practices require commitment, consistency and persistence before they become a healthy habit. We can therefore help ourselves to establish a supportive practice by considering our needs and aligning our healing intentions in accordance with our body's menstrual cycle (if we bleed), the phases of the Moon (if we do not bleed) or a combination of both in a way that feels comfortable and right.

# The Menstrual Cycle

The length of the female menstrual cycle varies from 21 days to 35 days, with the average being 28 days. Four key phases can be identified.

✳ **Days 1 to 5 – the menstrual phase**

On day 1 we begin to bleed. During menstruation, the womb lining is released, and we lose water. We often feel drained during menstruation, so this is a time for rest and recuperation. Yoni healing practices that help us feel open and relaxed and that support us with our release are recommended during menstruation. Yoni Self-Massage, with an external focus only, and Yoni Meditation are ideal. It's not a good idea to engage in Yoni Reflexology, Yoni Egg Mastery or Yoni Steaming while we are bleeding because our cervix is slightly open, making us a little more vulnerable physically and emotionally.

✳ **Days 6 to 10 – the follicular phase**

Once our bleeding is finished, our oestrogen levels begin to rise, an egg is ripening within our ovaries and the womb lining starts to thicken. Yoni healing practices with an intent to cleanse, energise and revitalise us are recommended during the follicular phase.

✳ **Days 11 to 18 – the ovulation phase**

When our oestrogen level peaks, an egg gets released into the fallopian tube. Many women feel a little bloated, notice their breasts are tender and observe changes in their vaginal discharge at ovulation. We might experience a sudden surge in libido, too. Yoni healing practices that heal, nurture and reawaken our sexual energy are recommended during the ovulation phase even if we don't intend to conceive.

✳ **Days 19 to 28 – the luteal phase**

Assuming we haven't conceived, our hormone levels drop during the luteal phase and the womb prepares for menstruation again. We may feel withdrawn and reflective during the luteal phase – many women struggle with mood swings as the tension builds before they bleed again. Yoni healing practices that help us engage with and understand our emotions, release pain and tension or restore balance are recommended during the luteal phase.

# The Moon

It's no coincidence that the Moon's 29-day cycle seems to mirror the female menstrual cycle and that many women's bodies seem to be naturally synchronised with the ebb and flow of the Moon.

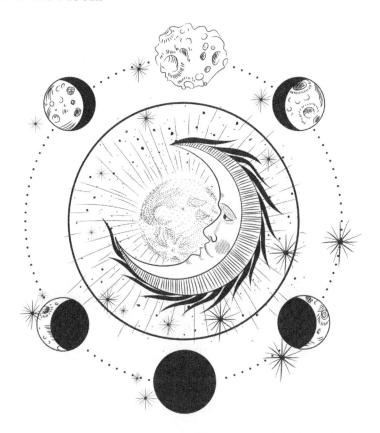

The Moon's energy amplifies our feelings. In Vedic Astrology, the Moon's position in our chart offers us insights into the nature of our deepest emotions. The Moon can also be thought of as a transmitter of karma. Since the key to understanding, transforming or transcending our karma lies in our emotional engagement with the challenges and lessons we encounter in life, working with the Moon can deliver wonderful results for many of us on a path of self-healing.

Some of us tend to bleed around the New Moon (white Moon cycle) and others around the Full Moon (red Moon cycle). We can encourage our cycle to synchronise with the Moon by connecting and communing with nature, developing a regular sleep pattern and by living in tune with the energies of the Moon as they shift and change through the lunar cycle.

✳ **New Moon**

**Menstruation (white moon cycle) or ovulation phase (red moon cycle)**

New Moon is the start of the lunar cycle. It's a perfect opportunity to withdraw into ourselves, to create space in readiness for new beginnings. When we rest and reflect on what's possible in our lives and relationships, we allow our soul to speak and inspire us.

✳ **Waxing Moon**

**Follicular phase (white moon cycle) or luteal phase (red moon cycle)**

Waxing Moon is the phase when the Moon appears to expand in size. This phase is for taking powerful action towards our highest desires, clearing away our obstacles and wielding our creative power.

✳ **Full Moon**

**Ovulation phase (white moon cycle) or menstruation (red moon cycle)**

At Full Moon we celebrate our successes and revel in our fullness. It's the perfect time to reap the rewards of the hard work that we've put in during the Waxing lunar phase and to be open to receive the blessings we desire. It's also a powerful time of release because emotional energy is amplified and everything we need to know or see is brightly illuminated.

✳ **Waning Moon**

**Luteal phase (white moon cycle) or follicular phase (red moon cycle)**

Waning Moon is the phase when the Moon appears to retreat, reducing in size as the sky darkens and we approach New Moon again. The Waning Moon phase is all about grateful reflection, healing and release. When we've mindfully rebalanced bodies and minds, we'll have integrated whatever occurred during this lunar cycle and be ready for another to begin.

# Create

## a sacred space

Yoni healing is a spiritually rich self-care practice, so the experience is always enhanced when we take a ritualistic approach and create a sacred space in the same way that we would if we were planning to meditate or work with spirit.

When we practice Yoni healing, we're communing with our own Inner Goddess, so it's helpful to consider how we can create a welcoming environment for this Divine aspect of ourselves to reveal herself to us.

# Make space

Privacy is usually really important. At first it may feel strange to tell our partner or family that we require some uninterrupted time to ourselves but in order to offer ourselves the attention that we need, it's vital to set a clear boundary. Our Inner Goddess may or may not be shy, but whatever the case, she's only prepared to show up on her own terms.

# Get organised

It's also a good idea to make sure that we have everything we need for our Yoni healing practices accessible – it's handy to set out our massage oils, essential oils, herbs and crystal tools in advance, making sure that everything is clean and ready to use.

# Create an ambient atmosphere

Creating a sacred space always begins with clearing the atmosphere. Simple ways to do this might be to open the windows for a short while to refresh the energy of the room, to burn some Palo Santo holy wood or to light a sage or incense stick and give the space a thorough smudge. Once a space is cleared, we can create the ambience that feels right for us. Many women prefer a dim, soft light because it feels safer and more comforting than bright light could ever be. Soft music also helps set a relaxing tone for Yoni healing.

# Invoke the Goddess

Finally, it's time to invite some spiritual support into the space. How we choose to do this might depend upon the nature of our faith or spiritual path. Yoni healing is a Divine Feminine art so it may feel right to light a candle and call upon a Goddess to whom you feel connected.

There are so many Goddesses, the beautiful, diverse

faces of the Divine Feminine, and so many different ancient spiritual traditions where the Goddess can be found. We may often find ourselves guided towards a particular Goddess because we resonate with her story and mythology. On other occasions we may not have an explanation for which Goddess steps forward – we simply hear her call.

**You are the temple.**
**Choose to become the sacred space.**

*—Rhian*

# Call upon

## Goddess Kali

There is one incredible Goddess whose essence takes us right to the core of the Divine Feminine – the Indian Goddess Kali.

Kali represents Shakti, the omnipresent, primordial, fertile, creative force. She is a dynamic Divine Mother archetype whom we call upon for transformation because she is associated with the eternal cycle of birth, death and rebirth and the creative feminine magic that inevitably propels us towards balance.

She is dark because she is protective and fearless, always taking us deep into the stillness of the void where we rediscover our power, potential and our truth. She is wild and liberated, unapologetically inspiring us to embody our desires. And her mythology tells us that she is also a victor in the name of pure love.

Kali is awake within us as Kundalini Shakti, the sacred, creative flow of sexual energy that elevates our consciousness from Root to Crown, burning through our fears and limitations, liberating us from our unhealthy attachments to the density of the past and reminding us that we know exactly how to magnetise our desires when we embrace our wholeness.

As such, she is the ultimate Divine Feminine healer. She restores our fullest feminine power.

There are many mantras that we can chant to help us connect with Kali, including 'om krim kalikaye namaha', which is traditionally chanted 108 times.

# The Kali Yantra

Kali is Yoni and Yoni is Kali. A Yantra is an ancient mystical diagram, encoded with sacred geometry, used in meditation and magic. Kali's Yantra captures the essence of Yoni with its downward triangle and central Bindu point that draws us to the core of creation.

Call upon Kali and meditate with her Yantra before Yoni healing. When we slow down our breath and focus on a Yantra, the archetypal energy encoded into the symbol is revealed to us and we are supported to become clearer about our own process.

During Yantra meditation, we focus our mind, release thoughts and eliminate distractions, so that the symbol can penetrate our deepest awareness. We're then able to conjure it up in our mind's eye at will and connect with its magical essence whenever we desire.

Goddess Kali speaks through her magical Yantra. When we listen to what she has to say we activate her presence within us and we allow ourselves to be Divinely guided towards true feminine power. We remember that we, ourselves, are a sacred space. We are lit up with Kali's Divine fire and we become determined and ready to heal.

**Kali transports you to the zero point –
the creative space where love and life
can be designed and redesigned on your
soul's terms.**

*—Rhian*

# Part Three

## Yoni Healing:
## The Practices

# Yoni
## breath meditation

The Yoni breath meditation is a foundational practice in Yoni healing.

It helps us leave the outside world behind and reconnect with ourselves so that we can become more present with and attuned to our Yoni. We become more grounded and centred, which makes Yoni breath meditation the perfect prelude to physical Yoni healing practices with the Yoni Egg or Yoni Wand.

In Yoni breath meditation we become more aware of our feminine centre and sensitive to our deepest needs. We may receive spiritual guidance or answers that we've been seeking about sex, relationships or our healing process. We start to feel more available to ourselves and open our Heart and Sacral Chakras as we expand feelings of gratitude and self-love.

When we include the Yoni Mudra (hand position) and work consciously with our breath, we set up a bio-electric circuit that our body and mind recognises, which calms the nervous system, boosts our intuition, supports the rebalance of the endocrine system and promotes a more peaceful, blissful state of mind.

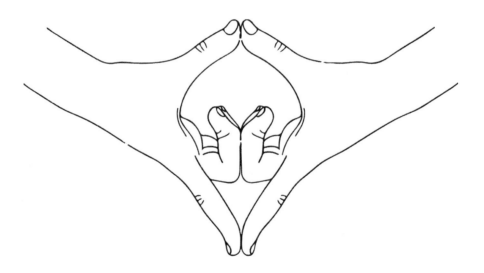

We can choose to make Yoni breath meditation a gentle, supportive practice or speed up the flow of our breath to make it a dynamic, energising experience.

# Yoni breath meditation step by step

✳ Sit cross-legged in the 'easy' yoga pose or on your knees. You can use a cushion or rolled up blanket to support yourself if it feels more comfortable. If neither of these positions work, sit on a straight-backed chair with your feet flat on the floor.

✳ Take a few deep belly breaths and form the Yoni Mudra, holding your hands in your lap over your lower abdomen. Make sure you're relaxed because holding a Mudra with too much tension will distract you from your meditation. If you do become distracted during the meditation, simply focus on the connection between your fingertips as you hold the Yoni Mudra. This will help you restore a sense of presence.

✳ Close your eyes and start to sense the pattern of your breath as you calm and clear your mind. Create a continuous circuit of breathing deep into the belly that becomes slow and steady.

✳ Focus on your Heart Chakra and visualise it opening and expanding. Generate a feeling of gratitude for yourself as your Heart Chakra is activated.

✳ Now focus on your Yoni and allow your breath to open and activate your Sacral Chakra.

✳ After a few more belly breaths, begin to contract and release your pelvic floor muscles in synchronisation with your inhales and exhales.

✳ On the inhale contract your Yoni. On the exhale release your Yoni.

✳ Keep going – after a while, it will feel like you're breathing with your Yoni.

✳ Lose yourself in the feeling. Work your Yoni muscles gently and breathe deeply.

✳ There's no need to rush. Take a break if you need to rest – simply continue breathing without contracting and relaxing your Yoni, returning to the practice when you're ready.

✳   After ten minutes or so, relax your Yoni and place your palms over your lower belly, forming a downward triangle shape.

✳   Stay connected to the pattern of your breath, tune into your Yoni lovingly and allow her to speak. Be open to receive her message. What does she want to tell you? What wisdom does she have to share with you today? If you don't receive a message, then ask your Yoni how she feels or what she needs.

✳   When your meditation is finished, open your eyes slowly and take your time to adjust to the light.

✳   Use the moments after Yoni Meditation to relax, reflect or journal. You may want to focus on your journey of healing, your path of self-love or how you're choosing to release the past, transform your relationships and create a more fulfilling future.

# Yoni

## reconnection

Healers and self-help experts always teach that it's vital to support our transformation by aligning our thoughts with our desired goal.

In the case of Yoni healing, we can use Yoni affirmations and Yoni gazing to boost our self-worth, foster more profound self-love and consolidate loving acceptance of our female body.

When we've spent a long time allowing our minds to spiral out of control with negative self-talk or we've become accustomed to criticism, our self-image is eroded and we feel unworthy.

Unfortunately, we women tend to inherit body image hang-ups from our mothers. We also develop shame and guilt about our Yoni through cultural conditioning because we're bombarded with false ideas about how a female body should look, smell, feel or be, despite the truth that every woman is unique and perfect.

Natural physical changes that occur due to pregnancy and birth, weight gain and loss or movement through different phases of life can create insecurities that contribute to the negative things we say and believe about ourselves.

Women who've endured sexual disrespect through abuse can also struggle to love and accept their Yoni. In fact, many women have learned to feel repulsed by their Yoni and this contributes to feelings of self-hate, a sense of disconnection from the feminine and sexual problems that can have a long-term, devastating impact.

# Yoni affirmations

Yoni affirmations are not a complete fix for deep-seated psychological issues, but they are a great self-help tool for us when we want to take control over the way we speak to ourselves, breaking that toxic cycle of self-berating.

Affirmations work best when used repetitively – repeat for five to fifteen minutes up to three times per day. It's also important that we invest emotional energy into them.

Their power is amplified when we say them to ourselves lovingly in the mirror as well as when we're relaxed or in a good mood.

Some women enjoy working with affirmations first thing in the morning and last thing at night. Others like to say them before or after Yoni breath meditation or during their Yoni healing practices.

We can write our own affirmations or find examples that resonate with us because they seem to address the issues we're struggling with.

*My Yoni is the Divine temple of my Inner Goddess.*
*I love worshipping my Yoni.*
*My Yoni radiates beauty, magnetism and power.*
*I love everything about my Yoni.*
*My Yoni is alive with creativity.*
*My Yoni is awake and I love her.*
*My Yoni speaks the highest truths.*

*I love listening to the wisdom of my Yoni.*

*My Yoni is receptive to love and pleasure.*

*I am discovering what brings my Yoni joy and bliss.*

*My Yoni deserves to feel juicy and abundant.*

*I love giving my Yoni exactly what she desires.*

*My Yoni is beautiful and perfect.*

*I am grateful for the wisdom, pleasure and magic of my Yoni.*

# Yoni gazing step by step

The practice of Yoni gazing is powerful when combined with Yoni affirmations. In fact, looking at our Yoni in the mirror helps us to release feminine shame and foster self-love and self-acceptance.

✱ To practice Yoni gazing, sit naked in front of a mirror with your legs apart so that you can see your Yoni. Soften your eyes so that you're looking at your Yoni with compassion and love.

✱ If Yoni gazing feels uncomfortable, send a beam of pure love energy from your Heart Chakra to your Yoni and choose to explore and acknowledge her beauty.

✱ Start repeating your chosen Yoni affirmations, expanding that feeling of love and acceptance in your Heart Chakra with each repetition.

# Yoni

## self-massage

Yoni self-massage is a wonderful way for us to get to know our body and discover new things about our sensuality. It's best approached mindfully and curiously with a sense of reverence and self-honour.

We are free to set our own pace for the experience and we don't need to worry about being self-conscious or pleasing another person. This makes Yoni self-massage incredibly healing and relaxing. It's a beautiful way to discover how we can give love and attention to ourselves.

Yoni self-massage helps us learn more about what makes us feel good and we can experiment with different kinds of touch and pressure to awaken our Yoni. It's up to us to choose whether we'd like the massage to be internal or not – sometimes we may prefer external self-massage and that's absolutely okay.

In addition to increasing our self-acceptance and fostering a better relationship between ourself and our Yoni, this form of massage offers us all the benefits of regular massage because it increases blood flow to the tissue of the Yoni, clears toxins via the flow of lymph and improves skin and muscle tone.

We're always advised to be gentle with ourselves when we practice Yoni self-massage because it can trigger emotional release, especially if we're holding pain or trauma in our feminine centre.

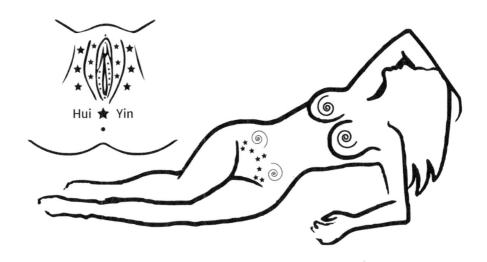

Hui ★ Yin

# Yoni self-massage step by step

✳ Set aside some private time when you won't be interrupted. Enjoy a relaxing bath or shower and create a safe, nurturing, sacred atmosphere that pleases you.

✳ Use an unscented, natural oil for your Yoni self-massage. Olive, sesame or coconut are ideal.

✳ Begin by finding a comfortable position, taking some deep breaths and clearing your mind. Remember to approach your Yoni self-massage lovingly and mindfully, observing, honouring and respecting your body. It can help to spend a few minutes breathing slowly with your hand over your Heart Chakra to form a loving connection with yourself.

✳ Use gentle strokes that feel comfortable to massage your breasts with both hands in a spiralling motion, clockwise and then anticlockwise.

✳ Do the same on your lower belly around the location of your ovaries. This loosens up and releases feminine energy and increases the feel-good factor. Don't rush because you're preparing your body for an intense experience.

✳ Move to the points indicated on the diagrams, all around your pelvic and pubic area. There are some important acu-points here that benefit women's health and vital energy flow. The Hui Yin is a major acu-point that stimulates the release and flow of sexual energy. Pay special attention to this point. It is located at the Root Chakra, the seat of the Kundalini. This is where your sexual flow will begin.

✳ Apply pressure with your fingertips and palms. Try longer, softer strokes too. Experiment with what feels really sensual. Areas of tension may need a firmer touch and more attention. Gentle pressure helps release blockages and shift stagnant energy.

✳ If you'd like your Yoni self-massage to be internal, start with gentle exploration using your fingers. You may choose to use a little oil for lubrication, or your natural juices may be enough.

✳ Relax and breathe deeply. Vocalise if you want to. Remain loving and self-compassionate about the experience.

✳ Slowly move your fingers around as if tracing the face of a clock so that you can mindfully and sensually explore the walls of your Yoni.

✳ Notice any areas of pain, numbness or tension. These areas may benefit from a little gentle pressure or softer, slower strokes – don't shy away from massaging them. You may trigger unusual sensations and tears may fall if you begin to release trapped emotions. Take your time and allow the emotions to flow because this is all part of your healing.

✳ If you want to bring yourself to orgasm then this is all good but it's not the aim of Yoni self-massage. It's helpful to take the pressure off yourself by not having any expectations of the experience. Make the only aim to stay present and meet your healing needs.

✳ When your Yoni self-massage feels complete, cover yourself with a blanket or shawl and relax in silence for a little while. Make the most of these moments of reflection or just enjoy some peaceful integration time.

✳ If you'd like to journal or make notes about anything that comes up for you to process, be sure that you feel ready before you put pen to paper.

# Yoni reflexology

Yoni reflexology is an extension to Yoni self-massage. The ancient Taoist teachings map the body organs to different areas of the Yoni.

When we massage and apply gentle, rhythmic pressure to these areas using fingers or a crystal Yoni Wand, the corresponding body organs and chakra centres are stimulated and revitalised. The Taoist teachings also suggest that particular positions during partnered sex will offer the same benefits.

Crystal Yoni Wands of various shapes and sizes can be purchased online. They can also be used as natural self-pleasure tools. They can be chosen intuitively or for their healing and metaphysical properties. Always choose a Yoni Wand with a softly polished, rounded end. If a wand arrives chipped, cracked or with a jagged surface return it to the seller for a replacement.

# Crystal choices

**Rose Quartz** *promotes self-love and relaxation.*
**Jade** *enhances sexual sensitivity and sexual healing.*
**Labradorite** *helps us understand the nature and purpose of feminine wounds.*
**Carnelian** *boosts sexual confidence.*
**Citrine** *promotes body positivity and enhances libido.*
**Aventurine** *supports emotional release.*
**Quartz** *amplifies good feelings.*
**Smoky Quartz** *releases trauma, negativity, fear or attachment to the past.*
**Amethyst** *enhances intuition and connection to the Inner Goddess.*
**Obsidian** *releases guilt and shame and facilitates dark feminine shadow work.*

Yoni Wands must always be cleaned before and after use. They can be cleansed energetically in running water and charged, just like other crystals, under the Full Moon.

# Yoni reflexology map

Areas of the Yoni can be mapped to organs of the body and its systems, the glands and the chakra system. The ideas below are not absolute – different systems of complementary healing may offer their own correspondences and interpretations.

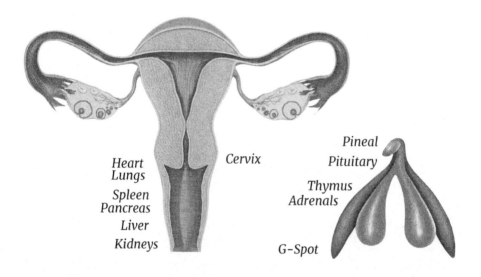

In addition, each of us is unique and we must not forget the power of our intuition and discernment when approaching our healing.

We could therefore decide that a 'map' isn't really needed and simply engage with the emotions and feelings that we tap into while self-healing with our Yoni wand. Our Yoni guides us as needed and it is up to us what meaning we choose to take from our personal experiences.

# The chakras and the body

**Root chakra** *mapped to the cervix, corresponds to the skeletal system and excretory system.*

**Sacral chakra** *corresponds to the reproductive system, immune system, spleen and adrenals.*

**Solar Plexus chakra** *corresponds to the digestive system, liver and pancreas.*

**Heart chakra** *corresponds to the circulation system, heart, lungs and thymus gland.*

**Throat chakra** *mapped to the G-spot, corresponds to the respiratory system and the thyroid gland.*

**Third Eye chakra** *corresponds to the eyes, brain and pituitary gland.*

**Crown chakra** *corresponds to the nervous system, spine and pineal gland.*

# Yoni reflexology step by step

* Create your sacred space, enjoy a bath or shower and begin with a luxurious Yoni self-massage.

* Before penetrating the Yoni with your crystal wand, form a connection with it by holding it over your Heart or Sacral Chakra, inhaling and exhaling slowly and deeply. Allow the crystal to become warm in the palm of your hand and have the sense that you're befriending and blessing it.

* Introduce your Yoni Wand to your Yoni slowly and mindfully. Be sure that your Yoni feels ready and willing – remember to breathe and relax.

* Yoni reflexology promotes emotional release in the same way that Yoni self-massage does. It's important to notice any areas of the Yoni that feel tender, painful or numb. Apply gentle rhythmic pressure to these areas, set the intention to release the emotion and pay attention to the thoughts and feelings that arise as you massage your Yoni.

* When we allow painful memories to surface, we can choose to let them go. It's okay to cry or moan. In fact,

vocal expression is often a vital aspect of emotional release, so don't hold back.

✳ Yoni reflexology can be intense, so set your own pace and do not feel pressured to tackle every area that requires attention in one session. You have plenty of time and it helps to heal in layers and stages so that you don't become emotionally overwhelmed.

✳ When your experience is complete, cover yourself with a blanket or shawl and take some time to rest and process. Enjoy a nap if you need to. Allow yourself plenty of integration time before you decide to reflect, process or journal.

**Self-healing leads to self-knowledge and self-liberation. Let Yoni lead the way.**

—Rhian

# Yoni
## egg mastery

The Yoni egg is a Taoist sexual health tool intended to tone, strengthen, heal and revitalise the Yoni.

Yoni egg practice involves cultivating the muscles of the Yoni and pelvic floor, referred to in the ancient Taoist teachings as the 'chi muscles'. Some of these muscles can be voluntarily moved while others aren't consciously controlled. The practice also strengthens the diaphragm and abdomen.

It activates the Hui Yin point on the perineum so that when sexual energy builds, a woman can consciously channel and circulate this flow. According to Taoist teachings, sexual energy can be harnessed to heal the internal body organs. It can also be channelled during alchemical sex to super charge our manifesting prowess.

Yoni egg practice isn't just about toning the muscles of the Yoni. It awakens, sensitises and heals the Yoni. It offers holistic health benefits because the internal sexual reflexology points are stimulated by the pressure of the egg.

Yoni eggs are traditionally carved from Jade. The ancient Taoists believed Jade to be a sacred feminine stone that soothes the Yoni, heals the reproductive system and balances the sexual energy.

Nephrite Jade is a dense, dark green stone that Crystal Healers associate with vitality and prosperity. It's said to energise the kidneys and heal the Heart Chakra. This is preferable to the light-coloured Jade that's available in abundance online. Unfortunately, this is an inferior quality stone that Crystal Healers might consider to have a weaker energy than Nephrite Jade.

Yoni eggs carved from a variety of healing gemstones can be purchased online. They can be chosen intuitively or selected for their healing and metaphysical properties. Many women choose Rose Quartz because it has such a gentle, loving quality. Others prefer Carnelian because it boosts the libido. Alternatively, Obsidian can support shadow work or the release of sorrow and negativity.

Yoni eggs have a pre-drilled hole through which it's possible to thread some plain, unflavoured dental floss. This offers the user peace of mind that the egg will be easy to remove.

They are available individually in three sizes or sets of three. Larger eggs are easier to feel inside the Yoni, but it's important to feel comfortable. Choosing to purchase a set of three Yoni eggs means that it's possible to start with the largest egg and progress to the smaller sizes as the Yoni muscles become stronger and more toned.

Contrary to some information available online, it's not a good idea to sleep with a Yoni egg inside the Yoni. The weight of the Yoni egg could place unnecessary pressure on the delicate walls of the Yoni and a woman cannot consciously grip the Yoni egg while she's sleeping.

Of course, it's important to keep Yoni eggs clean. It's been suggested that boiling them keeps them sterile. Alternatively, they can be washed well in hot water with a few drops of tea tree essential oil. Always remember to rinse Yoni eggs well because essential oil can be strong.

It can take a considerable amount of time and patience to achieve Yoni egg mastery and it's not going to be helpful to become frustrated when your practice challenges you. It's definitely counterproductive to speak harshly to your body or tell yourself that you'll never be able to master your Yoni egg.

You are not in competition with other women and how advanced your Yoni egg practice is says nothing about whether you're a good lover or how sexy you are.

Just accept where you're at with your practice and be compassionate with yourself. In time, with consistency and persistence, your Yoni will become stronger and you'll feel like you have more control over your muscles. No matter how far you come with your practice, continuing to work with your Yoni egg three times a week will benefit your feminine well-being and vitality.

# Yoni egg practice step by step

## stage 1

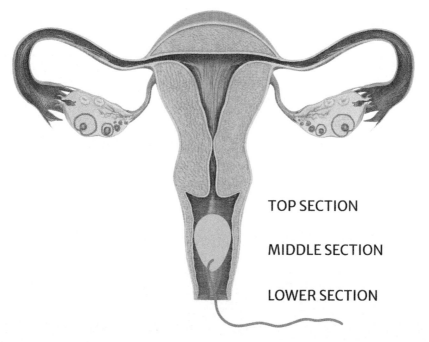

TOP SECTION

MIDDLE SECTION

LOWER SECTION

✱   Set up a private, relaxed atmosphere for your Yoni egg
practice. Begin by enjoying a Yoni self-massage.

✱   Spend a few moments forming a spiritual connection
with your Yoni egg, perhaps holding it over your Heart
or Sacral Chakra and breathing deeply. Offer your Yoni
egg a blessing of gratitude and love.

✱   If you have a specific healing intention that you'd like your Yoni egg to support you with, focus on it now. Crystal holds, conducts and emits energy, so your Yoni egg is a powerful healing tool.

✱ Insert the Yoni egg gently with the widest part first, keeping your breath slow and steady.

✱ The Taoist teachings suggest standing with your feet slightly wider than hip distance apart and your knees slightly bent when you use your Yoni egg. However, it's totally normal for women who are new to the practice to find that their Yoni egg falls out when they are standing up.

✱ If this applies to you then adopt a semi-reclined position with your hips slightly tilted. Alternatively, you can sit cross-legged in the 'easy' yoga pose if you prefer. You can progress to the standing position when your Yoni muscles have strengthened.

✱ Visualise the muscles of your Yoni in three distinct sections – top, middle and lower. With practice, these muscles can be isolated and contracted at will. When you're moving your Yoni muscles, use focus, visualisation and deep, belly breathing – trust you're in communication with your Yoni and that she's learning to cooperate with you.

* Contract the lower section of muscles, followed by the top, then the middle. Inhale slowly and deeply into your belly as you contract the muscles.

* When you contract the middle section of your Yoni, aim to grasp the Yoni egg. Use focus, intention and breath to move the Yoni egg up and down using the middle section of muscles, first slowly and mindfully, before progressing to a faster pace. This builds your vital energy.

* Rest and repeat up to nine times. Feel your energy build during the resting phase. Once you're confident with this practice, you can move onto stage two.

* An additional exercise is to inhale, clench your Yoni egg and tug on the string to provide some resistance. Rest and repeat again nine times.

* You can also try reclining on your back, inhaling and lifting the pelvis while using your Yoni muscles to pull your Yoni egg up towards the cervix, pushing it back down the Yoni canal as you exhale and relax. Always rest and repeat nine times.

# Yoni egg practice step by step

## stage 2

The Yoni muscles don't just have three sections. They also have a left and a right side that can be contracted independently with focus and intention. You'll need to develop your awareness of this and practice your ability to contract each side of your Yoni at will.

The Taoist teachings remind us that the stronger we make our focus and visualisation, the easier this stage of practice will be. It's the power of the mind that helps the many involuntary muscles in the Yoni to work in tandem with the voluntary ones.

This second stage of your Yoni egg practice has two parts.

✳ First, practice moving your Yoni egg from side to side by just using the top set of muscles.

✳ Next, practice moving your Yoni egg from side to side using the lower set of muscles. This will require you to contract the left and right sides of your Yoni independently, while contracting the top and lower sets of muscles in isolation.

✳ Rest and repeat nine times. Feel the energy build during the resting phase.

✳ Once you're confident with stage two, you can move onto the next stage.

# Yoni egg practice step by step

## stage 3

✳ Contract both the top and lower sections of your Yoni and move your Yoni egg from side to side using both sets of muscles together.

✳ Rest and repeat nine times. Feel the energy build during the resting phase. Once you're confident with this, you can move onto stage four.

# Yoni egg practice step by step

## stage 4

✳ Using both the top and lower sections of your Yoni muscles and continuing to work with your breath, use your skill to tilt your Yoni egg forwards and backwards.

✱   Rest and repeat nine times. Feel the energy build during the resting phase.

# Complete Yoni egg mastery

You've fully mastered the Yoni egg when you can combine all four stages into one routine.

With regular practice, your Yoni may become strong enough to 'suck in' a Yoni egg when it's partially inserted at the Yoni entrance. It's also possible to practice with two Yoni eggs and use your toned muscles to push them apart.

When you're confident with the large Yoni egg, progress to smaller sizes. Greater muscle tone is required to grip and move the smaller Yoni eggs.

You may become so familiar with your Yoni egg practices that you can make the muscular contractions as you go about your day even without the presence of a Yoni egg.

**Yoni egg is for all Yonis,
not just for Yogis!**

*—Rhian*

# *Yoni* steaming

Yoni steaming is a holistic self-care treatment that supports feminine wellness using a gentle, warm steam infused with herbs applied to the Yoni. It's recommended once weekly during the premenstrual phase of our cycle but contraindicated while we're bleeding.

As with many other holistic treatments, there's no scientific evidence to support claims that Yoni steaming alleviates menstrual cramps and bloating, rebalances hormones or cleanses the Yoni. However, we cannot deny that many women say they adore Yoni steaming and believe it to be supportive, healing and transformational.

Energy healing and emotional release are also benefits

reported with Yoni steaming that might be especially attractive if we've previously suffered women's health problems or feminine trauma.

Taking time to enjoy this relaxing, luxurious treatment truly feels like self-care. Giving our feminine centre some much deserved, focused attention feels wonderful. We become increasingly aware of our needs, embrace greater self-honour and create a stronger connection with our female body. And don't forget that a healthy, happy Yoni is wide awake, which means a juicier, sexually vibrant version of ourselves begins to emerge.

# Herbs for Yoni steaming

There are many different herbs that are suitable for Yoni steaming. Each has their own properties and application. Mugwort and Motherwort offer general benefits for menstruation and uterine health. To get started, here's a basic list of additional herbs worth considering. It's also possible to buy ready mixed packs of herbs on the internet from Yoni steaming practitioners.

|  | Chamomile | Raspberry leaf | Lavender | Rose petals | Calendula | Oregano | Basil | Sage | Rosemary |
|---|---|---|---|---|---|---|---|---|---|
| Vitality and circulation |  |  |  |  |  | ✳ | ✳ |  | ✳ |
| Healthy menstruation |  |  |  |  |  | ✳ | ✳ |  | ✳ |
| To cleanse and detoxify |  |  | ✳ |  |  | ✳ |  |  | ✳ |
| Antiseptic |  |  | ✳ |  | ✳ | ✳ |  |  | ✳ |
| Anti-inflammatory | ✳ |  |  |  | ✳ |  |  |  |  |
| To soothe and calm | ✳ | ✳ | ✳ | ✳ | ✳ |  |  |  |  |
| To tonify and relax |  | ✳ |  |  |  |  |  |  |  |
| Astringent |  |  |  | ✳ |  |  | ✳ | ✳ |  |
| To cleanse and heal | ✳ |  | ✳ | ✳ |  |  | ✳ | ✳ |  |

# Yoni steaming step by step

✳    Use two generous handfuls of fresh organic herbs or a big cup of dry herbs. It's best to source organic herbs to avoid exposure to toxins from pesticides or chemicals.

✳    Steep your herbs for an hour or so in a large, covered pan of boiled water the day before your Yoni steam and keep this covered overnight. This allows the natural oils and nutrients in the herbs to infuse into the water, creating a powerful healing potion for your Yoni.

✳    Yoni steaming is a healing ritual. Meditate before your Yoni steam, connect with yourself and call in spiritual support from Kali or another favourite Goddess, if you prefer. Some women like to call upon Artemis, the

Ancient Greek Goddess of the wilderness and to give thanks for the blessings of nature since Yoni steaming is a herbal treatment.

✳ Reheat your herbal infusion to boiling point but be aware that you must allow it to cool to a tolerable temperature before use. Always test the temperature of the steam. Your Yoni is delicate and burning yourself isn't part of the plan.

✳ When the steam feels temperate enough you can either place your pan beneath a slatted chair or stool or find a comfortable position on the floor that allows you to direct the steam towards your Yoni. You may need to improvise in order to find a way that works for you.

✳ This may involve squatting over the pan or sitting back on your buttocks with the pan placed between your open legs. Enclose the space around your lower body with a canopy of warm towels so that the steam cannot escape.

✳ It's possible to buy seats and stools online especially designed for Yoni steaming, but don't let the fact you haven't got one stop you from improvising.

✳ Relax and breathe deeply for 20 to 30 minutes while

the herbal steam works its magic. Enjoy the sensation of the warm steam on your Yoni. This is your time for release, cleansing and healing.

✳ After 20 to 30 minutes, move your pan to one side and take a further 20 minutes to rest and settle, reclining somewhere cosy and warm.

✳ You may feel drawn to meditate during this time. Deep breathing aids your relaxation. Remember this is a spiritual and emotional experience as well as a physical self-care practice, so make space for yourself on every level.

✳ After your Yoni steam, give thanks to Kali or Artemis. If you wish, offer your herbs back to Mother Earth.

Artemis, empower me with your courage.
May I return to my wild nature.

—Rhian

# Yoni
## care

There are so many misconceptions amongst women around how to care for our Yoni. It suits the women's healthcare industry to try to sell us all kinds of scents and soaps that they claim are formulated to benefit our well-being and sexual health, when in actual fact these harsh products can strip our Yoni of her natural balance and contribute to problems like bacterial vaginosis and other skin issues.

The truth is that our Yoni is self-cleaning. We don't need chemical soaps, douches, powders or scents to keep our Yoni happy. Washing our Yoni regularly with warm water, using natural products and taking the occasional epsom or

Himalayan salt bath is really all that we need to do.

Other things we can do to make sure that we have a happy, healthy Yoni include:

✳ Choose only cotton underwear because man-made fibres can cause irritation.

✳ Avoid nylon tights and leggings because they can encourage a combination of heat and moisture to become trapped near the Yoni, which becomes a breeding ground for bacteria.

✳ Seek out natural, unscented detergent to wash bedding and clothes.

✳ Use unbleached or plain white toilet tissue and avoid medicated toilet wipes, feminine hygiene wipes or baby wipes.

✳ Read the ingredients of personal products like lubricants and massage oils. Sometimes when we ask ourselves if we really need and want these products near our Yoni, the answer is no. Consider natural alternatives that are kinder to the Yoni and far more pleasant.

✳ Check out the wide variety of sanitary products on the

market. Some women prefer organic cotton tampons while others choose a Moon cup – it's a very personal choice and the important thing is to be informed about the pros, cons and environmental impact of each option.

✳ Consider natural alternatives to medications and pharmaceuticals where possible. It's important that we take care of our physical health and, of course, if we have concerns about our body then a physician must always be our first port of call. But complementary solutions like Homeopathy, Acupuncture and Aromatherapy also offer women viable alternatives and we all have the right to make an informed personal choice.

✳ Research how to use essential oils to optimise feminine well-being. It's widely accepted that tea tree, lavender and rosemary oils can support Yoni wellness. They promote a healthy vaginal environment and tackle yeast infections. For topical use it's important to dilute essential oils in a liberal amount of carrier oil – like organic coconut oil – because the Yoni is very sensitive.

✳ Eat optimal nutrition and be sure to remain hydrated. This can really make a difference to the quality, quantity and scent of our Yoni's natural juices.

✳ Finally, if there's an opportunity to visit the nudist beach or some other place where you'd feel safe and comfortable naked, try the practice of 'sunning' when the weather's favourable. You may have laughed at memes posted on social media about this, but you never know how great something feels until you try it for yourself! We can absorb the warmth of the sun through our Yoni, visualising her 'drinking' the light. Many women say this feels joyful and relaxing. It also balances and revitalises our cool, feminine Yin energy with the warmer, masculine Yang energy that's naturally present in sunlight.

# Your free gift

As a thank you for purchasing this book, you're being gifted access to Rhian's Yoni Healing Meditation package. Simply visit **bit.ly/yonibook** and enter your name and email to receive your login details and access the magic.

# Rhian Kivits

Rhian is an exclusive, one of a kind Love Alchemist who helps women heal, rise and love again after heartbreak, narcissistic abuse and toxic relationships.

With an international client base, she combines her solid background as a Relate trained Sex and Relationship Therapist and Urban Tantra Professional with all things mind, body and soul, especially Sacred Feminine spirituality.

Inspired by her own journey of healing and self-discovery after a traumatic childhood and history of painful relationships, Rhian shares the alchemical codes of self-awareness, self-love, self-expression and pleasure that heal the heart and restore the sacred blueprint of mind, body and soul so that women can finally move forward to find real love and embrace their life purpose.

Rhian has a passion for energy and gem medicine, sacred voice and sound activation, mudra and mantra meditation and Vedic Astrology.

As an initiate of the ancient Kundalini and Egyptian mystery school lineages and a trained Breathwork instructor, her gifts awaken the mysterious secrets of your sensual energy so that you can reclaim your entitlement to pleasure and fulfilment.

Rhian's clients love her mind-blowing combination of intuitive, psychotherapeutic insight, conscious relationship and sacred sexuality education and soulful activation that creates profound transformation and healing.

# Stay connected

bit.ly/freealchemy

www.rhiankivits.com

namaste@rhiankivits.com

www.facebook.com/rhianamykivits

www.instagram.com/rhiankivitslovealchemist

www.youtube.com/c/RhianKivitsLoveAlchemist

Printed in Great Britain
by Amazon

64518472R00071